Growing Toward God

LIFE LESSONS INSPIRED BY
THE WONDERFUL WORDS OF KIDS

Growing Toward God

DOREEN WRIGHT BLOMSTRAND
& BARBARA J. KOSHAR

Growing Toward God: Life Lessons Inspired by the Wonderful Words of Kids

© 2008 by Doreen Wright Blomstrand and Barbara J. Koshar

Published by Kregel Publications, a division of Kregel, Inc., P.O. Box 2607, Grand Rapids, MI 49501.

Library of Congress Cataloging-in-Publication Data
Blomstrand, Doreen Wright.
Growing toward God : life lessons inspired by the wonderful words of kids / by Doreen Wright Blomstrand and Barbara J. Koshar.
    p. cm.
1. Mothers—Prayers and devotions. 2. Grandmothers—Prayers and devotions. 3. Christian life—Anecdotes.
I. Koshar, Barbara J. II. Title.
BV4847.B53   2008   242—dc22   2008027347

ISBN 978-0-8254-4186-8

Printed in the United States of America

08 09 10 11 12 / 5 4 3 2 1

Children are a gift from the LORD.
PSALM 127:3 NLT

For our precious gifts:
Cindy Reynolds, Heidi Thomas,
Jace Blomstrand (1959–1996)

ဢ

Sara Guzzo, Renae Koshar,
Alexandra Koshar

Contents

Foreword, Jeannie St. John Taylor · 13

Acknowledgments · 15

Introduction · 17

1. God Fixed It · 19
2. A Child's Faith · 21
3. Love Never Fails · 23
4. Looking for Heaven · 25
5. Not to Worry · 27
6. Master Designer · 29
7. One Step at a Time · 31
8. Hurry, Honk, or Pray · 33
9. A Glimpse of Heaven · 35
10. One of a Kind · 37
11. Forget Me Not · 39
12. Open Line · 41
13. A Temporary Pleasure · 43
14. I'll Be There · 45
15. We Are Not Alone · 47

16. Father Knows Best · 49
17. A Call to Prayer · 51
18. Why Are They Weeds? · 53
19. Our Hope · 55
20. The Cheerful Giver · 57
21. Eyes of Faith · 59
22. The Lord's Handiwork · 61
23. Out of My Hands · 63
24. A Picture of Love · 65
25. Different by Design · 67
26. Where Are You? · 69
27. Where Can We Be? · 71
28. Love One Another · 73
29. Depend on Me? · 75
30. Ears to Hear · 77
31. Before the Sun Sets · 79
32. Ready, Set, Go · 81
33. In the Shadow of His Wings · 83
34. In His Image · 85
35. Learn to Listen · 87
36. Help in Troubled Times · 89
37. Heavenly Reunion · 91
38. Wash It Away · 93
39. Simply Content · 95
40. Pass It Along · 97
41. Forgive and Forget · 99
42. Can You See Me Now? · 101
43. According to What Is Done · 103
44. The Heart of a Matter · 105
45. A Wrong Assumption · 107

46. Joy in the World   ·   109
47. God's Word Stands Forever   ·   111
48. Worthy of a Smile   ·   113
49. White as Snow   ·   115
50. The Road to Heaven   ·   117

Foreword

My three-year-old son's normally glossy dark hair looked dull and felt gummy. "What'd you wash your hair with, Tev?" I asked.

"I didn't wash my hair. Tori helped me."

I directed a questioning look at his sister, barely sixteen months older than Tevin. "We used that stuff you spray," Tori told me.

My mind blanked for a moment. "You washed it with hairspray?"

"No. The stuff you spray that looks like hand lotion," Tori said.

I did a quick mental inventory of the bottles beside the tub. "Hmmm. Shaving gel?" I bent down to sniff Tevin's hair. "Yep. You used shaving gel. Smells pretty good. We might want to stick to shampoo in the future, though. Okay?"

They both cheerfully agreed; no more experimenting.

My two youngest children are grown now and Tori uses expensive salon shampoo on her long hair while Tev reserves the shaving gel for his chin. And yet I haven't forgotten that incident from their childhood; I smile every time I remember it.

But I have to admit I've never thought of it as more than a cute story.

We're all charmed and sometimes startled by the unexpected words and actions of children, but it takes someone of insight and wisdom to look beneath the surface and recognize deeper levels of meaning in the things youngsters say and do.

Doreen Blomstrand and Barbara Koshar are two such people. God has gifted them with the ability to perceive the spiritual concepts hidden in words of innocence. While the rest of us might appreciate a heartwarming story on a superficial level, these two women view it with spiritual eyes. They recognize biblical concepts and remember related Scripture. Then linking those precepts to profound quotes from well-respected Christians, they weave the individual threads into a rich tapestry embroidered with practical applications for daily life.

In this book, Blomstrand and Koshar share truth in a memorable, easy-to-understand way that will keep you turning the pages. So grab a cup of coffee, curl up in a corner of the couch, and begin *Growing Toward God.*

JEANNIE ST. JOHN TAYLOR
author of *Culture-Proof Kids: Building Character in
Your Children* and *How to Be a Praying Mom*;
author and illustrator of *Am I Praying, How I Pray for
My Friends,* and many other books

Acknowledgments

We're amazed at how God works and guides our lives as we venture into new challenges and how he holds us close during discouraging detours. A magnificent part of the journey is the people we meet along the way. We value all who assisted us while we wrote *Growing Toward God*.

We are grateful for each person who shared with us wonderful words from the "mouths of babes." To the children whose words made us smile: we're so glad that kids say delightful things and sometimes God speaks through you. Thanks for helping us discover many life lessons. Although not all the anecdotes we received made it into this book, we appreciate everyone who contributed. Our selections came from: Mary Ammann; Joyce Bica; Evelyn Boardman; Sondi Brown; Frances Dayee; Debra Fisher; Judy Groen; Kathy Harding; Lydia E. Harris; Betsy Hayford; Carolyn Israelson; Rena' R. Jugovic; Christine Merritt; Ann Morrow; Linda Noon; Donna Oiland; Cindy Reynolds; Patty

Sabandal; Carol Savage; Barbara Shea; Sheryl Solberg; Janis Stenka; Heidi Thomas; Viviane B. Thorpe; Rick Whitney; Bill, Jenny, and Christopher Wilson; Sherwood E. Wirt; Melissa Wright; and Lee Youk.

We're thankful to Pastors Jim and Betsey Hayford for taking the time to listen, share wisdom, and encourage us. We're indebted to Sherwood "Woody" E. Wirt and Christine Merritt for your kind support; we miss and will always cherish the morning coffee and critique meetings at Larry's Market. Our special thanks to Peggy King Anderson and Agnes Lawless for sharing your writing expertise and giving us wise suggestions. Yes, it takes time; it was worth it. Lydia Harris and our current critique group, we are grateful for your prayers and thoughtful assistance. Laurie Winslow Sargent, we're blessed by your enthusiasm and encouragement. Carla Williams and our NCWA friends, thanks for the inspiration you've added to the journey.

It's a joy and honor to work with the gracious team at Kregel Publications. We appreciate your guidance and expertise.

We express heartfelt appreciation to our families. You saw us through to the finish—we love you.

Our deepest love and gratitude go to our God. Thank you, Lord, for the comfort of knowing our times are in your hands (Psalm 31:15), and for acting on our behalf while we waited (Isaiah 64:4). We are so blessed that your Word is a lamp to our feet and a light for our path (Psalm 119:105).

Introduction

Let the little children come to me,
and do not hinder them, for the kingdom of
God belongs to such as these.

MARK 10:14

The words of children can be cute, witty, and wonderful, but spiritually valuable?

Yes!

We believe God uses everyday occurrences to teach us, and we've discovered whispers from heaven in the entertaining and sometimes poignant words of kids. In *Growing Toward God* we share our insights and struggles as we offer encouragement for life's challenges.

Our prayer is that these heartwarming anecdotes paired with Scripture will put a smile in your heart, edify your spirit, and leave you with the hope of an amazing eternity.

Growing together with you,

DOREEN AND BARBARA

I

God Fixed It

BARBARA KOSHAR

He will defend the afflicted among the people. . . .
He will endure as long as the sun,
as long as the moon, through all generations.

PSALM 72:4–5

When my daughter Alexandra was tiny, we occasionally said good night to the moon and twinkle stars. Wrapping her in a blanket, I'd take her outside and we'd spend a few moments observing the magnificent night sky. When she was two, we stepped outside one spring evening to see a pale yellow moon that was brilliant and fully round. Alexandra must have remembered an earlier moon that was only a half or crescent, because she studied the stunning full moon and exclaimed, "Look, Mom—God fixed it!"

I hugged my child and paused to enjoy the moment. Isn't it wonderful how God delivers lessons through little ones?

It had felt as though our lives had been covered by shadows

for several years. We'd been dealing with a serious illness and a spunky teenager while caring for a toddler. I was exhausted and sometimes only saw a sliver of hope shining through our difficulties. Yet that night, through the words of my young child, God reminded me that he was there.

I pondered the analogy and was comforted. In this great universe, it's amazing that God, who created the heavens, the moon, and all the stars, knows my name—and comforts me when I'm weary.

ഇ

Thank you, God, that your glorious light endures, even though I sometimes have difficulty seeing it when my eyes are veiled by challenging circumstances. Help me to trust you completely in all the hardships I encounter. In your time, in your way, you will fix it.

2

A Child's Faith

DOREEN BLOMSTRAND

This is the confidence we have in approaching
God: that if we ask anything according to his
will, he hears us.

1 JOHN 5:14

My third-grade granddaughter, Amy, won her class spelling bee. Her victory led to her participating in a countywide spelling bee at Central Washington University.

On the day of the contest, Amy was nervous. Her mother, Cindy, encouraged her to ask God to calm her fears and bring to her mind the words she had studied.

Horrified at the suggestion, Amy said, "Oh, Mom, I can't do that. It would be cheating."

"How would it be cheating?" her mom asked, perplexed.

Amy looked surprised at the question and replied, "Because God would be helping me."

Her mom and I were amazed at her response. Oh, for the faith of a child! To be certain that calling on God would give her such an unfair advantage, it would be cheating.

Believing that God is *able* to grant what I pray for is never a problem. Yet sometimes I have a problem believing he will do it for me. I know it's right to pray, expecting the answer. Still, I'm often surprised when I receive the miracle of answered prayer. A shadow of doubt may limit my expectation, but in no way does it limit a limitless God.

℘

Thank you, God, for the encouragement of Amy's faith. May my faith grow into simple childlike trust in you that will keep my prayers in line with your will. May my faith encourage others.

3

Love Never Fails

BARBARA KOSHAR

Love never fails.
1 CORINTHIANS 13:8

"My eyesight is weak, and my writing is poor," Seely's elderly aunt lamented. "I can no longer send letters and thank-you cards. I can't drive to visit my family; I don't even have the money to send gifts."

Nine-year-old Seely listened and tenderly replied to her great-aunt, "But you can still give your love."

At this innocent explanation, the woman's eyes filled with tears, and she replied, "You're right; I can."

I, too, sometimes see what I *can't* do more easily than what I can. Just like Seely's dear aunt, I often think, *If only I had . . . then I would . . .* Yet one thing we can always give is love.

After Paul wrote to the Corinthians about the importance of love, he defined it:

Love is patient, love is kind. It does not envy, it does not boast, it is not proud. It is not rude, it is not self-seeking, it is not easily angered. . . . It always protects, always trusts, always hopes, always perseveres. Love never fails. (1 Corinthians 13:4–5, 7–8)

So the next time I'm frustrated, I'll do my best to demonstrate love—remember to smile and show patience to someone who needs it. I can also watch for ways to show kindness to family, friends, and even unsuspecting strangers. And in tough situations, I'll pray to persevere with love. How?

I can do everything through him who gives me strength. (Philippians 4:13)

જી

God, help me see and respond to opportunities where I can share your love daily.

4

Looking for Heaven

DOREEN BLOMSTRAND

Those who seek the LORD lack no good thing.
PSALM 34:10

"This is a beautiful day for a flight," said Benjamin's mom. It was four-year-old Benjamin's first flight, and his mom, Carolyn, held his hand as they boarded the plane for Phoenix. Benjamin was happy it was a clear day and that he had a window seat. As the plane lifted off and gained altitude, Benjamin looked out the window.

When the plane was above the clouds, he pressed his nose against the glass and looked intently in all directions. Not taking his eyes away from the window, he continued peering out, searching the sky.

"What are you looking for?" his mom questioned.

Without glancing back, he answered, "I'm looking for heaven, where God lives."

When Carolyn told me this story, it reminded me what a

privilege it is to share God's truth with a child and to see such unquestioning faith. Yes, God lives in heaven, but he also lives in those who choose to trust him. Oh, that with such faith I would look for God in my daily life.

> Now faith is being sure of what we hope for and certain
> of what we do not see. (Hebrews 11:1)

The Practice and Presence of God records Brother Lawrence's words: "It is only faith that makes me know Him as He is. By means of it, I learn more about Him in a short time than I would learn in many years in the schools." Like many things, faith grows with regular practice in looking for God.

ജ

Father, help me to look for you daily with my whole heart and child-like faith.

5

Not to Worry

BARBARA KOSHAR

*Therefore do not worry about tomorrow, for
tomorrow will worry about itself.*
MATTHEW 6:34

Tears streamed down the second-grader's face as she entered the classroom with her fists tightly closed.

"What's wrong?" her teacher asked with concern.

Opening one fist, then the other, she sniffled and said, "My mom gave me a quarter for milk and a quarter for popcorn—and I forgot which was which."

This story reminds me of the many times I've worried unnecessarily.

Jesus reminds us not to worry. His words paint a lovely picture of his concern for us and tell us where our focus should be:

> See how the lilies of the field grow. They do not labor
> or spin. Yet I tell you that not even Solomon in all his

splendor was dressed like one of these. . . . Do not worry, saying, "What shall we eat?" or "What shall we drink?" or "What shall we wear?" . . . Your heavenly Father knows that you need them. But seek first his kingdom and his righteousness, and all these things will be given to you as well. (Matthew 6:28–29, 31–33)

Jesus is not teaching that we shouldn't work, but he's illustrating that if we seek God first, he will provide. If we have faith in our heavenly Father, we'll find peace and contentment, and not endlessly chase after things we don't need.

When panicky feelings threaten to steal my peace, I can envision the lilies I've planted in my garden. I'm always dazzled by their arrival in summer. And even in winter when dormant, the lilies rest and store strength for next year's elegant blooms. These words, attributed to Corrie ten Boom, remind me to be calm: "Worry does not empty tomorrow of its sorrow—it empties today of its strength." Now, that's wisdom we can hold onto tightly.

&

Help me to seek you, God, to rest contentedly, and to trust you for all my needs.

6

Master Designer

DOREEN BLOMSTRAND

Know that the LORD is God.
It is he who made us, and we are his.
PSALM 100:3

"Let's talk about what God made, Grandma," said three-year-old Brandon, buckled-up in the back seat of the car. "He made me."

"Yes, he did, Brandon," his grandma replied.

"He made you, Grandma."

"Yes, he did, Brandon."

"He colored you, Grandma."

"Yes, he did," Grandma said smiling.

Brandon exclaimed, "Hey, Grandma, God stays in the lines!"

On hearing Brandon's conclusion, I thought how beautifully God designs the colors and draws the boundary lines for what he creates. Brandon gave me a deeper way to look at how God uses colors and "stays in the lines."

The lines God has drawn are all around us, and we are acutely aware when something or someone steps over the line. An earthquake at sea causes a tsunami, and the ocean moves across its boundary lines, destroying everything in its path. Farmers cultivate between the rows because straying outside would destroy the crops. God's Word draws lines around our behavior. When we step over the lines, we suffer the consequences and may hurt others.

The Master Designer leaves nothing to chance. Psalm 16:6 says, "The boundary lines have fallen for me in pleasant places."

∽

Dear God, help me stay within the lines you have drawn for me and to see your creation with a childlike view—simple, direct, and fresh.

7

One Step at a Time

BARBARA KOSHAR

Go to the ant . . . ;
consider its ways and be wise!
It has no commander,
no overseer or ruler,
yet it stores its provisions in summer
and gathers its food at harvest.

PROVERBS 6:6–8

"Fold up your pajamas, and put them under your pillow," I instructed Alexandra. She had just graduated into her new "big girl" bed. "If you put them away each morning, then when it's bedtime, you'll always be able to find your jammies. They'll be right where you left them."

"Okay," she replied as her three-year-old hands fumbled with the pj's. She carefully placed her pillow on top of them and then went about her day. That evening as we prepared for bedtime, Alexandra peered under her pillow, pulled out her pajamas, and exclaimed with genuine amazement, "Look, Mom, it worked!"

Yes, consistent work habits reap rewards. Ants know this by instinct. We've all seen them marching one by one, carrying bugs or leaves larger than themselves while maintaining a harmonious cadence. Ants seem inspired from within. They know their purpose, and they get the job done.

Bruce Bickel and Stan Jantz, authors of *God Is in the Small Stuff and It All Matters*, write, "Over life's long haul, discipline works in every dimension of your life: financial, physical, mental and spiritual. If you've ever tried to get rich quick, tried to lose weight by taking a pill, tried to get knowledge by cramming at the last minute, or attempted to get close to God by asking for a miracle, you know what we're talking about." I know what they're talking about.

Yes, discipline works, but it isn't easy, especially for creative, free-spirited souls. My determination to get things done sometimes turns to discouragement, but that's when I need to remind myself, *with God's help, I can do this.* Then one day I, like little Alexandra, will be able to exclaim with delight, "It worked!"

∞

Thank you, God, for your example of the persistent, hard-working, and wise ant.

8

Hurry, Honk, or Pray

BARBARA KOSHAR

A man's wisdom gives him patience;
it is to his glory to overlook an offense.
PROVERBS 19:11

Joyce mooed, oinked, and quacked at Jenna, her three-year-old daughter. With each sound, Jenna named the farm animal. Then Joyce honked like a goose, "Honk, honk, hoooooonk. What makes that sound?" she asked.

Without hesitating, Jenna replied, "A car." Quite possibly Jenna had more often heard the honking of car horns than the honking of geese.

I've sure heard my share of car horns. One recent morning when I was driving, another driver honked his horn at me. Although the traffic arrow had turned yellow, several cars in front of me continued turning through the busy intersection. I stopped as the light turned red. A horn blasted. In my rearview mirror, I saw a young man in a yellow car make a nasty gesture at me.

I took a deep breath and muttered, "How dare you harass me for stopping at a red light!" After a long wait, the arrow turned green, and I turned left onto the roadway, now narrowed by construction cones. When the road widened, the harried driver speeded ahead, blaring his horn at me again.

When I told my sister this story, she said, "I'd have been tempted to stall my car alongside the construction workers to teach Mr. In-A-Hurry a lesson." We giggled at her response.

Revenge is a natural instinct, but God challenges us to do otherwise. Overlooking offenses isn't easy, and I haven't arrived. Yet I've learned one way to stay calm—say a prayer. It helps me cut the offender a little slack. Maybe the hurried driver woke late, burnt his toast, and stubbed his toe as he ran out the door that morning. Maybe he was rushing to the hospital because his child's condition just worsened.

It's a good thing to fill up with patience through prayer as we journey through life. And let's hope that others will have some patience for us when we're running near empty.

એૃ

Dear God, help me to be patient and to pray for those who offend me.

9

A Glimpse of Heaven

DOREEN BLOMSTRAND

*We have a building from God, an eternal house
in heaven, not built by human hands.*

2 CORINTHIANS 5:1

One summer while camping, four-year-old Andrew and his mom viewed the stars in the night sky. Their conversation turned from stars to heaven.

Andrew was full of questions. "Do we have to wear clothes in heaven? Will our dogs Klique and Arrow go to heaven when they die? Mom, when I go to heaven, can I sit on a cloud? Can I be an angel in heaven?"

His mother answered his questions as best she could.

Andrew grinned, "You know what, Mom? When I die, I'm going to have a lot of fun in heaven."

Like Andrew, most of us would like answers to our questions about heaven. Only one Source can provide the answers, and in the Bible he has given us just a peek of what heaven will be like. Jesus used parables to tell us about it. The book of Revelation gives us glimpses of an amazing heaven—from gates made of pearl, to streets paved with gold, to a crystal-clear river of life flowing from the throne of God.

Jesus offers comfort in words rich with promise:

> In my Father's house are many rooms; if it were not so, I would have told you. I am going there to prepare a place for you. And if I go and prepare a place for you, I will come back and take you to be with me that you also may be where I am. (John 14:2–3)

One thing we know for sure about heaven—we'll be living there with Jesus.

ॐ

Father, by your grace help me hold fast to the hope I have of one day seeing you face-to-face. Thank you for all you have prepared for me in heaven.

10

One of a Kind

DOREEN BLOMSTRAND

For you created my inmost being;
you knit me together in my mother's womb.
I praise you because I am fearfully and
wonderfully made;
your works are wonderful,
I know that full well.

PSALM 139:13–14

One day, three-year-old Jackson surprised his grandma. He jumped up from his quiet play and, with a serious face and determined step, marched up to her and announced, "I am who I am, and you're not. I am me."

Sharing this incident with me, his grandmother said, "I think it came from a sudden realization that he is himself and not me or anyone else. God also spoke to me that day through Jackson, reminding me that he is the great I AM, and I am not."

What empowering insight when a young child realizes his

separate identity. As I pondered Jackson's provocative words, I felt ashamed because I realized I sometimes act as though I were not wonderfully made. Instead I murmur, "Oh, God, why couldn't you have made me a little taller, a little prettier, a little more like someone else?" Like Jackson's grandmother, I need to be reminded that he is God, and I am not.

හ

Dear God, forgive me when I complain about how you formed me. I know your works are wonderful. Forgive me when I try to assume your role. Help me to remember that I am your workmanship, blessed with all I need, to be all you have planned for me.

11

Forget Me Not

BARBARA KOSHAR

*Can a mother forget the baby at her breast
and have no compassion on the child
she has borne? Though she may forget,
I will not forget you! See, I have engraved
you on the palms of my hands.*

ISAIAH 49:15–16

"I'll be your new Sunday school teacher," I told my three-year-old daughter Renae. I had just accepted the position at our church.

A puzzled and worried look crossed her face. "If you're going to be my Sunday school teacher, then who's going to be my mommy?"

I don't know, but we'll find someone nice, I was tempted to tease my vivacious daughter. Instead, I hugged her and said, "I'll always be your mommy."

This incident reminds me that God has many roles. He is our Father, but did you know that the Bible also attributes feminine characteristics to him? I now have to stop rolling my eyes at those who refer to "Mother God." In the Old Testament, God says,

> As a mother comforts her child, so will I comfort you. (Isaiah 66:13)

In the New Testament, Jesus said,

> O Jerusalem, Jerusalem . . . how often I have longed to gather your children together, as a hen gathers her chicks under her wings. (Luke 13:34)

I'll always think of God as "our Father in heaven," since that is how Jesus taught us to address him in prayer (Matthew 6:9). Yet it's comforting to know that God loves us with a nurturing heart—just like a devoted and affectionate mom.

℘

Thank you, God, that wherever I am, whatever I do, your compassion and unconditional love are there for me.

12

Open Line

DOREEN BLOMSTRAND

Call to me and I will answer you and tell you
great and unsearchable things you do not know.

JEREMIAH 33:3

One day soon after his grandfather died, two-and-a-half-year-old Taylor went downstairs to the family room. There, he sat cross-legged on the floor.

His mom peeked in and asked, "What are you doing?"

"I'm praying. I miss my grandpa, and I want to call him," Taylor answered. Then with hope in his voice, he added, "I wonder if Jesus has a telephone in heaven."

Well, there are no telephones in heaven. But we have a God who wants us to call him. Psalm 145:18 tells us, "The LORD is near to all who call on him." Phone lines and long-distance charges aren't concerns. We don't need to remember a number—just his name.

Connecting with God is easy; his line is always open. When

we call his name, we have a direct link to him with no answering machine and no assistant to screen calls. He is available 24/7.

> He who watches over you . . . will neither slumber nor sleep. (Psalm 121:3–4)

God not only listens when we call, he answers. He guides us, gives us wisdom, and brings clarity. With his help, we can make right choices and decisions.

ॐ

Father, thank you for always being available to take my call and for being happy to hear from me. Help me to keep my end of the line open—all day, every day.

13

A Temporary Pleasure

DOREEN BLOMSTRAND

*No temptation has seized you except what is
common to man. And God is faithful; he will not
let you be tempted beyond what you can bear. But
when you are tempted, he will also provide a way
out so that you can stand up under it.*

1 CORINTHIANS 10:13

Jenny and Bill pray with their two children, Ruth and Christopher, as they tuck them in bed each night. The children used to say the Lord's Prayer phrase-by-phrase after their parents.

One night when Christopher was three, Jenny and Bill came to "And lead us not into temptation . . ."

Christopher retorted, "I'm not saying that!"

He presumably had become aware of the fun that can be had from doing something he shouldn't. Like all of us, Christopher would have to learn that while sin may bring temporary pleasure, the pain of sin's consequences may last much longer.

As I encounter work-related challenges, struggles in relationships, and changing values in society, I need to remind myself to resist new temptations that come my way. When I think I've licked one, another may pop up to test what I've learned. Life is learn-and-grow.

৪০

Dear God, give me wisdom and strength to stand against the lure of temptations. Help me to be on guard and to recognize quickly when temptation sneaks up on me. Keep me aware that the consequences of sin usually far outweigh any momentary pleasure.

14

I'll Be There

BARBARA KOSHAR

*The LORD himself goes before you and will be
with you; he will never leave you nor forsake you.
Do not be afraid; do not be discouraged.*

DEUTERONOMY 31:8

One day little Becky was upset with her friend because Anna didn't want to play. Becky felt lonely.

Anna's mom explained, "Sometimes friends who spend a lot of time together get frustrated and need time apart."

Becky thought a bit and then responded, "Yeah, when my mom gets frustrated with my dad, he gets to have a good night's sleep on the couch!"

It's easy to feel alone, even when surrounded by people. Think of Moses and how lonely and discouraged he must have felt while leading the Israelites in the desert for forty years.

Moses wasn't alone, however. The first time God sent Moses to Pharaoh, the Lord assured the prophet,

I will be with you. (Exodus 3:12)

God had promised to lead the Israelites out of Egypt and give them a "land flowing with milk and honey" (Exodus 3:8). They experienced a miraculous escape and continuous provision; yet, in the desert, they felt forsaken. They whined, they rebelled, and they wanted to return to Egypt. Still, God's promise stood, and Moses reminded the Israelites that God would neither leave nor forsake them as they crossed the Jordan River to the Promised Land.

God is with us too. He will never leave or forsake us. Now that should inspire a good night's sleep.

80

Thank you, God, that you have promised to always be with me. I don't have to be fearful or lonely because wherever I am, you are there.

15

We Are Not Alone

DOREEN BLOMSTRAND

For where two or three come together in my name, there am I with them.

MATTHEW 18:20

Three-year-old Alexander and his mom, Christine, were picking up toys in his room. They stopped to share kisses and hugs, and Alexander enjoyed this time of closeness.

Seeing how happy her son was, his mom asked him, "How do you feel when we do this?"

Hugging her, he said, "I feel like someone else is here."

She kissed him and said, "There is! Jesus is here."

When Christine told me this story, I thought, *They experienced the presence of God in a very real way.* They felt his love, joy, and peace covering them that day.

I know that God, who has promised to be with me always, wants me to be aware daily of his nearness. In my active life, I sometimes forget that his promise never to leave me or forsake me means *never!*

He is always here in our midst. Perhaps we are never so aware of his presence as when, like Alexander and his mom, we are caught up in the spontaneous harmony of love.

ॐ

God, you are love. When I act in love, help me to realize your presence with me. In the routine of my daily life, let me stop to share love and to touch your heart by touching the heart of another.

16

Father Knows Best

Barbara Koshar

Hate what is evil; cling to what is good.

Romans 12:9

"Which pair of sunglasses are yours?" I asked my daughter Renae. Two nearly identical pairs rested side by side on the kitchen counter. Then I teased her, "We have matching sunglasses. Look, you bought sunglasses just like your mom's!"

"No, I didn't." Renae smiled as she continued the banter. "You bought sunglasses—just like mine."

As a teenager, the last thing my daughter wanted to admit to is being like her mom. But we are alike in many ways. We both enjoy the theatre, dislike balancing our checkbooks, savor turkey with stuffing, pass on hot dogs.

This reminds me that as a part of God's family, I should love what God loves and hate what he hates. And God does list the things he hates:

haughty eyes, a lying tongue, hands that shed innocent
blood, a heart that devises wicked schemes, feet that are
quick to rush into evil . . . and [anyone] who stirs up dissension. (Proverbs 6:16–19)

I don't spend time plotting wicked schemes to shed innocent
blood while concocting lies to cover my tracks. Yet I've stirred
up a pot or two of dissension. I've lapsed into behavior that's a
less-than-great example of Christianity. But with God's help I
can keep sin from becoming a habit I'm oblivious to. And how
grateful I am that God loves forgiveness!

In this process of growing toward God, I'm praying for eyes
like his, no rose-colored glasses that make light of sin, and no
dark shades to hide it, but clear vision to avoid evil and cling to
good. Yes, I want discerning eyes and a gracious heart—just like
his.

∽

*Father, help me to love what you love and cling to what you say is
good.*

17

A Call to Prayer

DOREEN BLOMSTRAND

Do not be anxious about anything, but in everything, by prayer and petition, with thanksgiving, present your requests to God.
PHILIPPIANS 4:6

"Look!" said my four-year-old granddaughter Ashley. It was early on a Sunday morning, and Ashley stared out the window as I drove by a park. "That man doesn't have a place to live, Grammy. I think he lives on the grass."

A man was curled up on the lawn. I slowed the car to a crawl to get a better look. It was a cold morning, but the man had no jacket. His shirt and pants looked dirty.

"What makes you think he doesn't have a home, Ashley?"

"Because I've seen him sleeping on the grass before when I was with Mommy."

Ashley and I talked about being homeless and how the one action we can always take is prayer. Then with some urgency, she said, "Grammy, you and me have to pray for that man."

So we did, all the way to church that Sunday morning. We don't know what happened to the man. We only saw him a few other times and then no more. We continued to pray for him whenever we passed the park or thought about the homeless.

Ashley's call to prayer helped me remember that when someone who has a need comes to my attention, God is asking me to pray. He is reminding me that he has chosen to work through prayer.

❧

Father, open my eyes to see the people and situations you put in my path. May I bring you pleasure by being quick to stop and pray.

18

Why Are They Weeds?

Barbara Koshar

Love each other as I have loved you.

John 15:12

"Don't you wish we had grass with flowers in it like they do?" four-year-old Drew exclaimed. He had spotted a lawn dotted with brilliant yellow dandelions during a walk with his mom.

Drew's mother, Debbie, just smiled. Dandelions are not welcome among her perennial gardens and carpets of smooth green lawn.

Why are dandelions disdained? They aren't prissy like roses. No thorns either. The cheerful buttons greet us each spring, shine all summer, and then waltz away on the autumn winds. Children love dandelions, and grown-ups don't. We just have different points of view.

God admonishes us to love one another as he loved us, but people, like plants, can be labeled *fragrant flowers* or *tenacious weeds*. Some people just don't fit into our preconceived notions.

Individuals with different backgrounds and values can make us feel uncomfortable. Stress or illness can lead some people to demonstrate perplexing behavior. And like dandelions that spring up on pristine landscapes, misunderstandings can pop up unexpectedly among family and friends.

My first inclination is to avoid those who annoy me—and vice versa, I'm sure. I'm realizing, though, how much my own personality influences my viewpoint. So now I'm challenged to pray a blessing for the difficult people I encounter, rather than to assume I should weed them out.

Mother Teresa summed it up beautifully: "If you judge people, you have no time to love them."

Well, now that I've made peace with dandelions, God, will you explain why you created slugs?

ଔ

Help me, God, to love and accept others as you love and accept me.

19

Our Hope

DOREEN BLOMSTRAND

Your . . . faith and love . . . spring from the
hope that is stored up for you in heaven and
that you have already heard about in the
word of truth, the gospel.

COLOSSIANS 1:4–5

Snuggled in bed, eight-year-old Brandon watched a movie with his grandma. He suddenly said, "Grandma, you're going to die."

"You're right, Brandon. Someday I'm going to die." Grandma Donna, who's been raising Brandon since his mother died, hugged him and reassured him of her love.

Soon after this conversation, Brandon asked, "Grandma, when you see my mommy in heaven, tell her I'm doing okay."

With a smile, his grandma hugged him again and said, "I will."

Brandon's faith in God's love and promise of eternal life reminds us of the hope we can all have:

a faith and knowledge resting on the hope of eternal life,
which God, who does not lie, promised before the beginning of time. (Titus 1:2)

Those words are an encouragement to me in keeping alive the
flame of hope in my heart. When it's my turn to move on to
heaven, I expect to see loved ones who are already there. What a
reunion we'll have!

෨

*Dear God, thank you for taking care of every detail of what is to
come. May I live here and now in the hope of what is to come, and
then throughout eternity in all you have prepared.*

20

The Cheerful Giver

BARBARA KOSHAR

Whoever sows generously will also reap generously.
Each man should give what he has decided
in his heart to give, not reluctantly or under
compulsion, for God loves a cheerful giver.

2 CORINTHIANS 9:6–7

As I sipped coffee and scanned the Sunday morning paper, my ten-year-old daughter Alex snuggled up next to me and asked, "What name do you like best, Bubbles or Rosemary?"

"Depends on the color. You'll know when you choose your bird," I replied.

"I need a few more dollars to buy my parakeet. Could I clean the bathrooms and fold towels to earn some money?" Alex asked.

"I cleaned the bathrooms yesterday and the towels are all folded."

"I'll mess them up and refold them," Alex offered.

"No thanks."

She persisted, "Do you need anything?"

"Yeah," I mumbled, "peace and quiet so I can read the newspaper."

A slight smile fluttered across her face. "Okay—five bucks?"

I sighed, shook my head, and gave Alex one of those "Mom needs a break" looks. She then let me relax and read. No bribe.

Later that week we visited my hometown. When we met Alex's grandpa for breakfast, he marched up to her with a grin and handed her a five dollar bill. Alex was delighted with the unexpected gift. She had been saving for months and now had just enough to buy the supplies and parakeet she'd been waiting for.

God whispered to me in that moment. My message to Alex had been work and save, and that's important. Yet, there is great pleasure in showing love with a spontaneous gift.

Did I need anything? Yes. I needed a reminder that God loves a joyful and generous heart.

ℰꙨ

Thank you, God, that you will provide all I need. Help me show my love to you and others by giving cheerfully.

P.S. We now enjoy Bubble's cheerful chirps. Thanks, Dad. We love you.

21

Eyes of Faith

DOREEN BLOMSTRAND

In his heart a man plans his course,
but the LORD determines his steps.

PROVERBS 16:9

One winter day, my daughter Cindy bundled up her three-year-old son to play in the snow. Matthew fidgeted and hopped from one foot to the other, eager for the adventure ahead. Dressed in a warm jacket, boots, and mittens with a stocking hat snug over his ears, he ran for the door.

A kiss and "have fun" sent him outside. As he charged ahead, he pulled the stocking hat down over his face.

"Wait!" his mom called. "Pull up your hat or you can't see where you're going."

Spinning toward her voice, he said, "It's okay, Mama. I'll just follow my feet."

Matthew's reply paints a vivid word picture of what God sometimes asks us to do—walk by faith. When we can't see what is ahead, simply follow.

God told Abraham to leave his home in Ur. By faith he left and started walking, unable to see where God wanted to take him.

We may have times when we feel God urges us to go, but we don't know where he is leading us. We can remember,

> If the LORD delights in a man's way, he makes his steps firm. (Psalm 37:23)

ഇ

God, help me walk in obedience when I can't see the whole picture; to follow where my feet take me, trusting you to guide my steps.

22

The Lord's Handiwork

DOREEN BLOMSTRAND

*For since the creation of the world God's
invisible qualities—his eternal power and divine
nature—have been clearly seen, being understood
from what has been made, so that men are
without excuse.*

ROMANS 1:20

On a camping trip in Yosemite Valley, seven-year-old Alexander and his parents sat around the campfire enjoying the warm, clear night. Alexander stood up to get ready to get into his sleeping bag, but stopped to look up.

Not taking his eyes off the picture of bright stars against black sky, he said, "You know, when you put all the stars together, they make one person—Jesus."

Scripture says that God is clearly seen in the things he has made. From starry skies to valleys low, God is visible in nature.

The heavens declare the glory of God; the skies proclaim the work of his hands. (Psalm 19:1)

Lift your eyes and look to the heavens: Who created all these? He who brings out the starry host one by one, and calls them each by name. Because of his great power and mighty strength, not one of them is missing. (Isaiah 40:26)

Alexander expressed an insight I sometimes miss in the rush of daily life. He saw Jesus in his handiwork. What a wonderful thought he carried to bed that night.

℘

Father, you've given the world so much beauty. Help me to slow down long enough to look, appreciate, and to give thanks for your visual masterpieces. Like Alexander, may I see the reality of who you are and see your attributes revealed when I look at what you have created.

23

Out of My Hands

BARBARA KOSHAR

Trust in the LORD with all your heart
and lean not on your own understanding;
in all your ways acknowledge him,
and he will make your paths straight.

PROVERBS 3:5–6

Baby Christina was savoring her favorite treat. But as she licked the vanilla ice cream, it tipped out of her cone and plopped onto the restaurant floor.

"Don't worry, Pee-wee," Grandpa assured Christina as he walked away.

But the child couldn't be comforted. Mom and Dad watched her sad expression turn to tears, then sobs.

One-year-old Christina didn't understand that Grandpa went to replace the cone. She could only focus on her loss. Her tears continued because she didn't see the complete picture.

This reminds me that God is a faithful Father and provider.

How priceless is your unfailing love! (Psalm 36:7)

David, who penned Psalm 36:7, had an amazing faith. When others ran in fear, this shepherd boy with a sling and a stone defeated a nine-foot, armor-clad giant with a bronze javelin slung on his back. Later, as king of Israel, David accepted circumstances, from abundance to heartache, because he knew God's love.

Martin Luther King Jr.'s words challenge us: "Faith is taking the first step even when you don't see the whole staircase." He couldn't have known the eventual outcome when he took his first step of protest against segregation.

Let's remember that God's love is unfailing. We can trust him with all our hearts, even when our sight is limited. Then we won't be so distressed about what slips out of our hands.

❧

God, thank you that I can trust you and transfer all my concerns from my hands into yours.

24

A Picture of Love

DOREEN BLOMSTRAND

*Those who plan what is good find love
and faithfulness.*

PROVERBS 14:22

One day four-year-old Christopher decided to draw a picture for his great-grandmother. She had died a year earlier, and Christopher and his mom had just talked about her.

When he finished, he said, "We should keep it until we die and go to heaven so we can give it to Nana." After thinking about it, he thought of a quicker way to deliver his gift to her. "Let's give it to our mailman so when *he* dies he can take it to heaven for her."

Although mail-delivery service doesn't exist between earth and heaven, God knows our desires, thoughts, and intentions. Nothing we plan surprises him, but he doesn't automatically turn them into actions. Doing them is our part.

Let us consider how we may spur one another on toward love and good deeds. (Hebrews 10:24)

Do not forget to do good and to share with others, for with such sacrifices God is pleased. (Hebrews 13:16)

Christopher's sweet intentions count as a good thing in God's book. And I am reminded not to put things off. Lives can change in a heartbeat, and I may not have another opportunity to act on my good intentions.

෩

Father, help me to act on good intentions in the present, and not lose the opportunities you provide to share good thoughts or deeds with others.

25

Different by Design

BARBARA KOSHAR

*We have different gifts, according to the
grace given us.*
ROMANS 12:6

"I e-mailed you my English paper. Can you look it over, especially the first paragraph?" my daughter Sara asked.

"Sure," I replied. "A strong beginning is important."

My college student quickly retorted, "I know, I know, and it needs to be better well-written."

We both giggled at her fumbled words, and I thought, *Yes, it may need to be "better well-written."* Yet Sara aces geometry and trigonometry, and I still count on my fingers.

God has given each member of my family different abilities. One of my grown daughters excels in language and the arts, the other in math and organization. One is an enthusiastic extrovert; the other has a serene personality. And number three right now is bubbly and fun, fun, fun. She naturally loves to run, climb, and dance. I don't think she'll be looking for a desk job when she grows up.

Although Romans 12:6 refers to spiritual gifts, it also illustrates God's ingenuity. He's given us diverse gifts, talents, and abilities. Everyone is different by design. When we discover who we are and find what we do best, we can work efficiently and serve others effectively. The secret to enjoying what you do is to do what you enjoy.

In the past, I struggled with my work, until I realized it didn't fit who I am. I've made changes, and I find passion and pleasure in most of what I now do, which includes figuring out how things can be "better well-written."

ℰↄ

Thank you, God, for the variety of gifts and talents you have given us. May I appreciate and honor the uniqueness of each person you have made.

26

Where Are You?

Doreen Blomstrand

I am the LORD, the God of Israel,
who summons you by name.
Isaiah 45:3

"Mommy, I think Grandma is saying, 'Andrew, where are you?'
and I said, 'I'm here, Grandma. I'm coming.'"

Three-year-old Andrew and his mother, Karen, were on their
way to visit his Grandma Lee, where Andrew was looking forward
to spending the day. He loved to see her and knew she would be
happy to see him.

What a wonderful example of what a right conversation with
God should be like. God says to us,

Call to me and I will answer you. (Jeremiah 33:3)

But when God calls our names, are we quick to say, like the
prophet Samuel, "Here I am; you called me"?

After Adam and Eve had eaten the forbidden fruit in the Garden of Eden, "The LORD God called to the man, 'Where are you?'

He answered, 'I heard you in the garden, and I was afraid because I was naked; so I hid'" (Genesis 3:9–10). Unlike Andrew in response to his grandma, Adam experienced guilt and fear when God called to him.

God knew where Adam was, so why did he ask the question? No doubt, God gave him the opportunity to respond, to come to him even though Adam was vulnerable in his current state.

When he calls, I can't hide from God either. He wants me to come, just as I am.

ॐ

Father, help me to hear when you call and to respond quickly as Samuel did when he said, "Speak, LORD, for your servant is listening" (1 Samuel 3:9). You promise to answer me when I call to you. Thank you for letting me know how much you value our conversations.

27

Where Can We Be?

BARBARA KOSHAR

My prayer is not that you take them out of the
world but that you protect them from the evil one.
JOHN 17:15

Grandma diligently swatted the flies swarming the picnic table.

Three-year-old Ellis seemed puzzled. He glanced up at her and asked, "Nana, why do you kill flies outside too? If they can't be inside, and they can't be outside, where can they be?"

I believe Ellis was asking, *Where can flies be safe?* We all want to feel safe, but we don't live in a completely safe world. We are swatted at. Internally, our own doubts and inadequacies attack our hearts. Externally, we suffer the consequences of our own sins and those of others. Where can we be safe?

Shortly before he left this earth, Jesus looked toward heaven and prayed for his disciples and for those who would believe through their message. He asked his Father to protect us from evil, to give us unity and joy.

Father, I want those you have given me to be with me where I am, and to see my glory. (John 17:24)

So while life may not always be a picnic, we can rest assured that God loves us. He has more compassion than even kind-hearted Ellis. With God—that is where we can be safe.

છ

Father, when I don't feel safe, may I follow Jesus' example of praying for protection. Thank you that you are with me.

28

Love One Another

DOREEN BLOMSTRAND

*Dear children, let us not love with words or
tongue but with actions and in truth.*

1 JOHN 3:18

"Mom, did you know that when I was little I put my pennies in
the trash can?" fourteen-year-old Sara asked her mother.

Amazed, her mom asked, "Really? Why did you do that?"

"So homeless people would find money to buy food when they
went through the garbage."

What a profound act of love this was for a preschool child. Not
only did Sara have compassion, but she acted on her concern for
the poor by sacrificing her pennies to do what she could to help.
Sara's story reminds me—God asks me to do what I can.

Did homeless people find any of her pennies? Probably not.
Did Sara's kindness count in God's ledger? Yes! Remember how
much Jesus valued the widow's sacrificial giving of two small cop-
per coins. It was all she had (Luke 21:2–4).

The words of C. S. Lewis in *Mere Christianity* also challenge us: "I am afraid the only safe rule is to give more than we can spare. If our charities do not at all pinch or hamper us, I should say they are too small."

Sometimes I may see a need but don't act because I think, *What little I can do won't matter.* God reminds me that love is more than what I say; love is what I do. The little things often matter most to him.

સ

Dear God, help me not to put off even the smallest act of love. Keep me aware that you care more about my motive than the size of my deed.

29

Depend on Me?

BARBARA KOSHAR

Make it your ambition to . . . work with your
hands . . . so that your daily life may win the
respect of outsiders and so that you will not be
dependent on anybody.

1 THESSALONIANS 4:11–12

"I'm going to take a shower now," my friend Carol told her two young daughters. She set full cereal bowls on the kitchen table for them and went upstairs. A few minutes later, Carol came down to retrieve her morning coffee. "Why aren't you eating your breakfast?" she asked the girls, who were quietly sitting at the table.

"We don't have spoons!" five-year-old Marissa answered.

Nine-year-old Ali laughed, and Carol had one of those "aha" moments as she realized she had been doing too much for her girls.

I, too, find it easy to do for others what they can do for themselves. I have to remind myself not to pick up my daughter's clothes or put her homework in her backpack. Doing too much for children, or even other adults, deprives them of opportunities to be dependable, hardworking, and mature. Scripture teaches us to take responsibility for ourselves and allow others the consequences of their choices.

> A sluggard does not plow in season; so at harvest time he looks but finds nothing. (Proverbs 20:4)

This proverb can be paraphrased—no work, no eat.

Now Carol says she encourages her girls to help with meals and to get their own snacks. She reports that they occasionally have an extra spill to clean up, but her lovely daughters are learning self-sufficiency.

֎

Help me, God, not to do for others what they can do for themselves.

30

Ears to Hear

DOREEN BLOMSTRAND

I heard and my heart pounded,
my lips quivered at the sound.

HABAKKUK 3:16

My granddaughter, two-year-old Tiffaney, and her parents were visiting us for the week. For the first time, she heard the siren that rang out loud and shrill in our town once a week at noon. Clapping her hands over her ears, Tiffaney cried, "My ears are scared!"

We hardly even notice it anymore, but it was an unexpected, scary sound to Tiffaney. Scooping her up, her grandpa comforted her and assured her that the siren would soon stop.

Tiffaney's reaction is how I feel about some language I hear on TV and in the movies. Those words not only "scare my ears" but assault my spirit. I fear that, just as we became accustomed to the siren, I might become so used to the flagrant use of foul language that it will lose its shock value. It hurts because it's not honoring to God.

Research has revealed that on TV programs at the eight o'clock prime-time hour, this type of talk has had a significant increase, and at nine o'clock it has increased even more. As our culture becomes more desensitized to hearing profane and obscene language, it continues to escalate.

ಕಾ

Dear God, I pray that as much as it is up to me, I will avoid listening to such language. Help me not to grow so calloused that I don't even notice it anymore. May it continue to "scare my ears."

31

Before the Sun Sets

BARBARA KOSHAR

*Do not let the sun go down while
you are still angry.*
EPHESIANS 4:26

Five-year-old Sam had ongoing tummy aches. To get him to volunteer information about his stomach, his doctor asked, "Sam, has something been bothering you lately that you'd like to tell me about?"

Sam pondered a minute then replied, "Yes, I have this tag in the back of my shirt that's really bugging me."

Don't you love the honesty of children? They live in the moment. If something is bothering them, they tell us—usually loud and clear. Yet many of us grown-ups tend to suppress angry feelings. Our stomachs churn, our shoulders tighten, and our temples throb, perhaps because of hurt feelings, a misunderstanding, or our unwillingness to forgive.

The Bible teaches us to take care of anger daily—before the

sun sets. Why? When we sleep with anger, we risk starting the next day frustrated with everyone, including the kids and the dog. And ignored anger multiplies. Spitefulness and mean-spiritedness are always delighted to join anger. That's why Scripture tells us:

> Get rid of all bitterness, rage and anger. . . . Be kind and compassionate to one another, forgiving each other, just as in Christ God forgave you. (Ephesians 4:31–32)

We all occasionally encounter difficult problems. Sometimes we need to step back and breathe deeply, cry, or seek counsel. We can overcome many obstacles, however, with honest prayers or sincere twilight chats. Don't keep putting on a shirt with a stiff tag that irritates. Take if off and deal with it—before the sun sets.

ॐ

Help us, God, to settle differences quickly with kindness, understanding, and forgiveness.

32

Ready, Set, Go

DOREEN BLOMSTRAND

So if the Son sets you free, you will be free indeed.
JOHN 8:36

Williston was four years old when his family moved to Brisbane, Australia. There, his father pastored a church.

On the Fourth of July that year, his mother gave to him a small American flag. She told him about America's fight for freedom in the Revolutionary War and said, "Our flag reminds us that we are a free people."

Williston took the flag when he went out to play with his friends.

"What's that flag you're waving?" one of his young playmates asked.

"That's the flag that makes you free," he said.

"Free to do what?" his friend asked.

Williston paused a minute, then in a serious tone replied, "Free to get ready and four to go."

81

When I think of Williston's call to action, I'm delighted with his funny, spontaneous response. But there is truth in his words. Gaining freedom requires *readiness* and a willing heart to *go* after it—to vote, to help a neighbor, to give support. Ready, set, go may be a call to action for anything—to serve others, to spend time with family, or to learn from a new experience.

True freedom, however, comes through Jesus Christ, who said,

> "You will know the truth, and the truth will set you free." (John 8:32)

෨

Help us, God, to desire the freedom you offer and to be ready to go after it with our whole hearts.

33

In the Shadow of His Wings

BARBARA KOSHAR

I will protect him, for he acknowledges my name.
PSALM 91:14

Eight-year-old Sara shared her gratitude before our Thanksgiving meal. "I'm thankful for my mom and dad, my little sister, and this yummy dinner," she said.

"And what are you thankful for, Renae?" I asked.

Five-year-old Renae sighed and then exclaimed, "I'm thankful that Tyrannosaurus rex is extinct."

Our family broke out in laughter at her response. Several weeks before, we had observed full-size dinosaur replicas at the science center. After viewing these giants, Renae was relieved to learn she couldn't be crushed beneath monstrous dinosaur feet because they no longer tromped the earth. Whew!

When I think of Renae's response, I, too, am thankful that I haven't had to face many of the gigantic disasters I often hear about. I have not successfully avoided them all, however. Difficult circumstances such as unemployment, serious illness, or the death of a loved one can seem like a Tyrannosaurus rex, seeking to shake our faith and stomp out our joy.

Paul challenged believers with these words:

> Be joyful always; pray continually; give thanks in all circumstances. (1 Thessalonians 5:16–18)

I wish adversity were extinct, but I've learned I can live through it by praying for protection and strength. I've also learned I need to thank family and friends who embrace me when I'm fatigued, and to thank God, who uses difficult times to teach me to trust him.

ℰ⊃

Thank you, God, that you keep me in the shadow of your wings. You have protected me from many disasters that I haven't seen, and you strengthen me in the difficult circumstances you allow.

34

In His Image

BARBARA KOSHAR

So God created man in his own image,
in the image of God he created him.

GENESIS 1:27

"What did God make?" Mary asked her little brother Adrian
after reading his Sunday school lesson to him. The lesson had
taught, "God made all things," yet six-year-old Adrian was silent and seemed puzzled. Mary then coached him: "Look out the
window. What do you see? Tell me what God has made."

Adrian glanced at the grove of fir and pine trees, the fruit-filled
orchard, and acres of mown hay. He looked near the farmhouse
and driveway, then in a voice filled with satisfaction he replied,
"Daddy's car."

Mary was surprised. This wasn't the answer she was looking
for, but after a moment she saw the truth in it. Mary expected
Adrian to focus on God's handiwork in creating people and nature. Instead, Adrian pointed out a human's creative mind and

industrious hands. Mary agreed; God did indeed provide the knowledge and materials to construct a car.

Just as a car is not a product of chance and probability, neither are we. Since God created us in his image, we are able to create. The process of creation remains a mystery. Yet when creativity and hard work join hands, the result is amazing beauty—Michelangelo's *The Creation of Adam* on the Sistine Chapel ceiling, an artistic English garden, and a fabulously designed car. How can we not see a glimpse of God in such imaginative craftsmanship?

∽

Help me, God, to identify and use my creativity in ways that honor you.

P.S. Mary treasured this moment she had with Adrian because several weeks later Adrian went to heaven to be with his Creator. (And since then, Adrian has greeted Mary there.)

35

Learn to Listen

BARBARA KOSHAR

There is a time for . . . every activity
under heaven: . . . a time to be silent and
a time to speak.
ECCLESIASTES 3:1, 7

"Please be quiet now. We want to talk." Rachel's grandmother kindly asked her chatty three-year-old granddaughter to stop jabbering so she could continue a discussion with her husband.

Rachel was silent for a short time while they spoke, but then she piped up, "You be quiet now. I want to talk."

Rachel's grandparents burst out laughing. I wonder if God sometimes feels this way about me. Do you ever envision him saying, "You be quiet now. I want to talk"? Talking to God is important. There is a time to be silent, however—to listen, reflect, and learn.

Do not be quick with your mouth, do not be hasty
in your heart to utter anything before God. God is in

heaven and you are on earth, so let your words be few.
(Ecclesiastes 5:2)

Jesus told his disciples not to babble prayers like the pagans, and he reassured them,

Your Father knows what you need before you ask him.
(Matthew 6:8)

Prayer should be a sincere, two-way conversation, not a routine or rushed monologue. How can we listen to God? We can know his voice by reading and meditating on his Word. Sometimes he speaks through others; sometimes he whispers to our hearts. How can we hear if we're never still?

Silence is often difficult. But next time I'm tempted to babble on, I pray I will stop and take time to listen.

෨

Father, help me to be still and know that you are God.

P.S. Advice from a bumper sticker: "Talk only if you can improve on the silence."

36

Help in Troubled Times

DOREEN BLOMSTRAND

God is our refuge and strength,
an ever-present help in trouble.

PSALM 46:1

Shortly after Thanksgiving, Tyler's dad called for a family meeting to discuss Christmas plans. He informed everyone that their presence would be required, with no excuses.

All were gathered except seven-year-old Tyler, who was still upstairs in his room. After waiting what he felt was a reasonable time, his dad went to get him. At the stairs he called, "Son, we need your presence in the living room."

Choking back tears, Tyler responded, "But Dad, I don't have any *presents*."

When Tyler's dad told me this story, I had mixed emotions. It was cute, funny, and also poignant. I smiled, but tears were close to spilling over when I thought of Tyler upstairs by himself, sad and worried because he should be at the meeting. Yet he couldn't go because his *presents* were required, and he had none!

Tyler's misunderstanding of a word reminded me of the small things I worry about. Tyler thought he was in an impossible situation. Stay or go, he would be in trouble either way. In reality, there was no problem, only the misunderstanding of a word, a small thing that his father would explain to him. With a smile, Tyler could join the rest of his family in the happy business of making Christmas plans.

My birth father is no longer here to calm me when I'm upset. But my heavenly Father is always with me. He helps me realize that my anxious thoughts often keep me from receiving his peace.

> Cast all your anxiety on him because he cares for you.
> (1 Peter 5:7)

What a good reminder!

℘

Father God, thank you for all the times you give peace to me and let me know I have nothing to fear.

37

Heavenly Reunion

DOREEN BLOMSTRAND

It is sown a natural body,
it is raised a spiritual body.

1 CORINTHIANS 15:44

When Jenny's father died, she explained to her five-year-old son, Christopher, "Granddad's now in heaven."

Christopher's confident response was, "With his boy!" And he was. Nearly four years earlier, Jenny's brother died in a car accident. Christopher doesn't remember him, but his family often talks about Uncle Jeremy. Christopher knows that he is in heaven.

Jenny was impressed that Christopher understood the relationship between his uncle and his grandfather. But she was even more impressed with Christopher's confidence of their place in heaven together.

The Bible indicates that our heavenly bodies will be different from our earthly ones, but we will recognize each other. What a comforting thought it is for us to know that our loved ones who died trusting God now see the face of Jesus. At the Last Supper, Jesus comforted his disciples:

> Before long, the world will not see me anymore, but you will see me. Because I live, you also will live. (John 14:19)

It seems we will also dine with others in heaven:

> Many will come from the east and the west, and will take their places at the feast with Abraham, Isaac and Jacob in the kingdom of heaven. (Matthew 8:11)

One day when I join them, loved ones will come to meet me, including my husband and son. Like Christopher's uncle, my boy is with his dad, and both are with our heavenly Father.

ꙮ

Dear God, thank you for the assurance that death doesn't mean oblivion but life to-be-continued.

38

Wash It Away

BARBARA KOSHAR

Create in me a pure heart, O God.
PSALM 51:10

"David" came in from recess, his pants covered with a thick coat of mud. "I fell down," the six-year-old kindergartener explained.

I was helping in the classroom, so the teacher asked me to take this little guy to the school office for a change of clothes. When he was finished, I folded up the muddy pants and placed them in a plastic bag. "Be sure and give these to your mom so she can wash them right away," I instructed the boy.

"Okay," he cheerfully responded. "I was going to put them in the wash anyway; my dog peed on them."

I hid my giggle and thought, *Bet his mom didn't know about the dog when she sent him to school today.* So the pants were only slightly soiled in this youngster's mind until the discomfort of cold, wet mud warranted a trip to the laundry.

This makes me wonder how easy it is to entertain negative

thoughts until they become grungy and uncomfortable, not only to us, but to those around us. Our hearts may tell us to change, but thoughts quickly become attitudes or habits that are difficult to shed. How can we keep clean hearts and minds?

Here's God's solution:

> Whatever is true, whatever is noble, whatever is right, whatever is pure, whatever is lovely, whatever is admirable—if anything is excellent or praiseworthy—think about such things. (Philippians 4:8)

If we replace resentful complaints or gloomy thoughts with lovely ones, our hearts and minds are more likely to be clean, fresh-scented, and stain-free.

&

God, help me to be quick to wash away negativity and to focus on the positive.

39

Simply Content

BARBARA KOSHAR

But godliness with contentment is great gain. . . .
But if we have food and clothing, we will be
content with that.
1 TIMOTHY 6:6–8

It was December. Every room in Debbie's comfortable home was festive. Cheerful snowmen, wreaths, and bows greeted visitors on the front porch. A lovely tree was selected and adorned. One day just after Christmas decorating, Debbie's charming three-year-old son Ryan surveyed the living room and declared, "The tree doesn't look nice without presents under it."

How easy for us to see what we don't have rather than be thankful for everything we do enjoy. This childlike dissatisfaction seems to be in us from birth, and it can push us to make positive changes. But contentment defined is "the state of being satisfied."

Am I satisfied with my possessions? Or do I glance about and grumble, "This doesn't look nice without . . ."

In his letter to the Philippians, Paul stated,

I have learned to be content. (Philippians 4:11)

In my effort to learn contentment, I'm thanking God for the simple blessings I don't always stop to appreciate: savory herbs and flavorful fresh fruit. Warm blankets and restful sleep. Eyes to take in the calming beauty of woodlands and oceans. Feet that carry me there.

These words from Rose Fitzgerald Kennedy's *Times to Remember* can inspire us to be satisfied: "Some of the greatest people in history have lived lives of the greatest simplicity. Remember, it's the you inside that counts."

∞

God, I wish not only to be content but to be genuinely thankful for the simple pleasures you've created. Each day may I appreciate your beauty, goodness, and provision.

40

Pass It Along

BARBARA KOSHAR

Be imitators of God . . . and live a life of love.
EPHESIANS 5:1–2

Joanna enjoyed imitating her big brother Jesse, who was a rambunctious five-year-old. But Jesse sometimes taught his little sis typical boy stuff that his mom didn't appreciate.

One day two-year-old Joanna wanted to pray before dinner. Her prayers were usually simple, a thank you and amen. So her parents were surprised when Joanna began, "Thank you for the rainbows and stars . . ." She continued to thank God for each person in the family and everything she could think of.

Jesse was pleased as he announced, "She learned that from me!" And she had. Jesse often began his detailed prayers with, "Thank you for the rainbows and stars . . ."

It's amazing how much our examples influence others for good—or not. I have a habit of not picking up the phone on the first ring, even if it's beside me. I'm not sure how or when I developed this practice, but it seems abrupt to answer immediately, so I usually wait for the second ring. One day the phone rang when it was next to my daughter. I watched as she glanced at it, let it ring again, and then picked it up. I'd never verbalized this habit, yet I had passed it along.

How many other habits do my children imitate? How many do I owe to my mom? What habits should I change? It's something to think about. Do I reflect God's love as best I can? Even if I don't realize it, my daughters are watching, and they may someday proclaim, "I learned that from Mom!" Will I be pleased, perplexed, or distressed?

∞

Help me, God, to imitate you and to be an example of your love.

41

Forgive and Forget

DOREEN BLOMSTRAND

*Clothe yourselves with compassion. . . . Forgive as
the Lord forgave you.*
COLOSSIANS 3:12–13

Six-year-old Brandon had a canker sore in his mouth. While helping him brush his teeth, his grandma bumped the sore and made it hurt. Later, she clipped his fingernails and accidentally clipped one too short, hurting his finger and causing him to pull away.

Getting ready for bed that night, Brandon said, "Grandma, you hurt me twice today."

"I know, Brandon, and I'm sorry. Will you forgive me?"

"I forgive you, Grandma. Now you don't ever have to say it again." Connecting his thumb and index finger to make the "okay" sign, he said, "It's all gone."

What a wise example of true forgiveness, unconditional and complete. I thought about times I was slow to forgive. Other times I forgave quickly but found forgetting difficult. Unlike Brandon, I wasn't quick to say, "It's all gone."

Brandon's words remind us of how God forgives and forgets.

> As far as the east is from the west, so far has he removed our transgressions from us. (Psalm 103:12)

> [God will] hurl all our iniquities into the depths of the sea. (Micah 7:19)

The illustration is often used: "Then God places a sign that says 'No Fishing!'" When I find it difficult to forgive and forget, I'm tempted to "go fishing." It helps to remember:

> Blessed is the man whose sin the Lord will never count against him. (Romans 4:8)

₞

Father, help me to forgive as you forgive and forget as you forget. I pray that through your enabling power, I will become more and more like you.

42

Can You See Me Now?

BARBARA KOSHAR

A man's ways are in full view of the Lord, and he
examines all his paths.

PROVERBS 5:21

Five-year-old Charlie needed to go potty. He didn't want to quit playing and go inside though. Instead, he tightly covered his eyes with his hands and then peed in the backyard.

His surprised mom corrected him.

Charlie looked bewildered and asked, "If I couldn't see you, how could you see me?"

When I was young, mothers in my neighborhood watched over the kids playing on the street, and the moms knew they were welcome to correct or tattle on unruly children. Sometimes my mom got a phone call. "How did you find out?" I'd ask when scolded.

My mom's usual reply was, "A little birdie told me."

Maybe this saying comes from Ecclesiastes 10:20: "A bird of

the air may carry your words." I quickly learned I couldn't get away with much.

Mom no longer disciplines me, of course, but God does. He knows my every thought, sees my every action, and even examines my motives. I don't have to ask, "How did you know?" God knows everything; and he knows whether I'm ignorant or disobedient.

> Do not forget my teaching, but keep my commands in your heart, for they will prolong your life many years and bring you prosperity. (Proverbs 3:1–2)

God watches over us and disciplines us because he wants us to benefit from his wisdom. The question is, are we listening to him, looking for him, and seeking his wisdom? Or do we sometimes cover our eyes and pretend he's not there?

ℂ

Father, open my eyes so I may see you and learn your wisdom.

43

According to What Is Done

DOREEN BLOMSTRAND

*Let your light shine before men, that they may see
your good deeds and praise your Father in heaven.*
MATTHEW 5:16

It was the last morning of a visit with our daughter and her family. We said good-bye to our seven-year-old grandson Cory as he left for school.

With his arm around Cory, my husband said, "Have a good day, Cory, and tell everyone at school how smart you are."

Before hurrying out the door, Cory turned and said, "I don't have to tell them, Grandpa. I'll just do the work, and then they'll know."

I smiled all that morning as I remembered Cory's words, but I also pondered an important Christian truth. Through Cory, God reminded me it is not who I say I am that speaks to the hearts of others, but it's what they see in my life. I want to embrace this truth daily: If I live it, I won't need to say it.

In "Thought Conditioners," Norman Vincent Peale wrote, "When you have done all that you can do, don't try to do any more, just 'stand.' Relax, stop, be quiet, don't fuss about it, stay calm; you have done everything possible; leave the results to God."

෪

Teach me, God, to be an expression of your love so others will see Jesus in me. Help me remember that others will know who I am, not by what I say, but by what I do.

44

The Heart of a Matter

DOREEN BLOMSTRAND

Man looks at the outward appearance, but the
LORD looks at the heart.

1 SAMUEL 16:7

Seven-year-old Jayme smiled at herself in the mirror. "Oh, you beautiful doll," she sang, "you great big beautiful doll." She hesitated, then sang out, "I don't know the rest of this song, but I don't care because I'm losing my hair."

And she was. Jayme has leukemia. Her treatment not only caused changes inside her body but it also caused changes in her outward appearance. But she was able to smile at herself and sing because she knew she was beautiful in God's eyes, despite what others might see.

Jayme has a wonderful attitude in the midst of a very difficult situation. It is a reminder that with God beside us, we can get through the hard places in life with positive attitudes. Her brave outlook reminds me of how often I look at outward appearances and worry what others think, rather than looking at the heart of a matter.

What we see may not be what God sees. He cares more about our motives and attitudes than what shows on the surface. While we may focus on our appearance, God is examining our hearts.

We are always beautiful to our Creator—like Jayme, who could smile at herself, because she is God's beautiful child.

ഇ

Teach me, God, to care less what others think and more about what you think. Help me to see with your eyes so I can know more of your heart in the circumstances of life.

45

A Wrong Assumption

DOREEN BLOMSTRAND

*It is not good to have zeal without knowledge,
nor to be hasty and miss the way.*

PROVERBS 19:2

Sandy's daddy was almost bald. One day as the two played together, he asked her, "What do you think happened to all my hair?"

Sandy reached out one small hand and patted her daddy's scruffy beard. She thought for a minute, then said with a bright smile, "It came out on your face."

Assumptions may be sweet and funny like Sandy's, but sometimes they can prove serious.

Numbers 22:21–33 tells us the story of Balaam, the mercenary prophet, and his donkey. God was angry with Balaam because of disobedience, and sent an angel to oppose him. His donkey saw the angel and turned away three times from the path where the angel stood. Since Balaam couldn't see the angel, he assumed his donkey was stubborn and beat him each time. But by avoiding the angel, the donkey, in fact, saved Balaam from harm.

I know how easy it is (and not just for a three-year-old) to come to hasty conclusions and make wrong assumptions. Before arriving in Southeast Asia to work in a refugee camp, I made negative assumptions about the location, the culture, and the work. I thought the camp would be dirty, the people distraught, the work depressing. I'm happy to say I was wrong. The camp was well organized, the people a joy to serve, and the work meaningful. I learned a valuable lesson and now am less quick to judge.

ॐ

Dear God, keep me from leaping to wrong conclusions and help me to acquire wisdom. "Teach me knowledge and good judgment" (Psalm 119:66).

46

Joy in the World

BARBARA KOSHAR

Our citizenship is in heaven.
PHILIPPIANS 3:20

Early one morning, two-year-old Alexandra begged her dad for some jelly beans. He shook his head no and replied, "Let's wait until after lunch to eat jelly beans. Do you want toast or cereal for breakfast?"

Immediately, Alexandra responded, "No, no, no, I don't want toast or cereal. I want lunch!"

Sometimes I'm like Alexandra when I tell God what I want and when I want it. And what do I want? To be happy! Don't you?

Yet are we confusing happiness with joy? Happiness is temporal. It's like getting jelly beans—or better yet, chocolate mocha truffles—before lunch. Melt-in-your-mouth richness that only lasts a moment. But joy is the hope we find in God.

My brother Jimmy taught me a lot about joy. Jim was in his

twenties when his joints began aching severely, and he was diagnosed with systemic lupus. After a few remissions, the disease conquered his kidneys, then attacked his brain. Yet during the fourteen years of battling this illness, Jim kept smiling. He worked when he could and rarely complained. When hospitalized, he took windup toys to amuse the nurses. Jim also turned to God; he read the psalms and the book of Job. He seemed to know his future was in heaven, and he died just before his fortieth birthday.

In the book of Revelation, the apostle John describes heaven:

> [God] will wipe every tear from their eyes. There will be no more death or mourning or crying or pain. (Revelation 21:4)

Jim wasn't always happy, and he didn't get the healthy body he wanted on earth, but God gave him patience to endure. He had a peace and joy that was hard to explain. I miss my brother, but I find joy in knowing that Jimmy's at home in heaven.

℘

Dear Father, when I'm in pain, remind me to look to you for hope, comfort, and joy.

47

God's Word Stands Forever

BARBARA KOSHAR

The grass withers and the flowers fall,
but the word of our God stands forever.

ISAIAH 40:8

"A nickel is worth five cents, and a dime is worth ten," Joyce explained to her curious three-year-old son Jesse. "And this is a quarter; it's worth twenty-five cents." She handed him the coin and added, "You can even make a phone call with a quarter."

Jesse immediately lifted the quarter to his ear and shouted, "Hello?"

Today Jesse doesn't need to carry change to make phone calls since cell phones have made pay phones nearly obsolete. Many things now become outdated quickly—yet the Bible remains a best-seller. Even though written over a span of 1,500 years by a diverse group from fishermen to kings, the Bible presents a harmonious theme of reconciliation between God and humanity.

While loved by many, the Bible is also hated. Throughout

history people have banned and burned Bibles, yet the Book survives. It's interesting, too, that even those who war against God likely follow his patterns. Our years are numbered from Christ's birth, and six days of work followed by a day of rest comes from Genesis, as does our institution of marriage. God's ways pulse throughout the earth.

Unbelievers may claim the Bible's principles are outdated. Yet, in many countries where Christians are persecuted, Bibles are smuggled and read in hiding. Pages are torn out and shared, and believers willingly choose death over denial. Human ideas and inventions will come and go, but God's Word remains unique and eternal.

∞

Thank you, Jesus, that you are "the same yesterday and today and forever" (Hebrews 13:8).

48

Worthy of a Smile

DOREEN BLOMSTRAND

*Light is shed upon the righteous
and joy on the upright in heart.*

PSALM 97:11

"I'm so happy!" three-year-old Hannah said. She stood gazing at the fleecy white clouds and flying fish mobiles dangling about her preschool classroom.

Her teacher Patty smiled and asked, "Why are you happy?"

"Because I like fish," Hannah answered.

How wonderful that Hannah can express happiness at seeing colorful, make-believe fish. If I'm observant, I, too, will notice little things that make for joyful moments.

As adults we often get busy, distracted, or grumpy and miss those small moments, those flying fish and fleecy clouds, that could result in spontaneous smiles.

In *Jesus, Man of Joy*, Sherwood Eliot Wirt wrote, "Joy is not a mere sentimental word. It has a clean tang and bite to it, the exhilaration of mountain air. That's because it blows away the dustiness of our days with a fresh breeze, and makes life more carefree."

How many times have we exchanged grins for grumbles? Life is too short to lose even one moment of delight. This is not to confuse deep, abiding joy in the Lord with circumstantial happiness. But it is a reminder not to miss the everyday things God gives us for our enjoyment.

A cheerful heart is good medicine. (Proverbs 17:22)

Studies now show that happiness helps us live longer. Smile—it's a good thing!

&

Dear God, help me stay in the present each day and be alert to the many little things that bring a happy state of mind.

49

White as Snow

BARBARA KOSHAR

"Come now, let us reason together,"
says the LORD.
"Though your sins are like scarlet,
they shall be as white as snow."
ISAIAH 1:18

Three-year-old Joshua romped through the backyard snow. He suddenly picked up a handful and put it in his mouth.

His mom disapproved, "Don't eat the snow! It's dirty."

"Then let's put it in the washing machine, Mom!" Joshua replied.

Joshua's comment reminds me of a favorite childhood memory. One winter night while visiting my grandfather's farm, I awoke, and a soft light drew me to the window. I peered between the curtains and was enchanted by a tranquil scene—in the moonlight, snowflakes fluttered onto slopes of white fields that were edged with frosted evergreen woods. I gazed out the window for a long time, absorbing the beauty of fresh snowfall in the pristine Idaho woods. This wasn't city snow, which needed washing; it was pure country snow. This is the snapshot I see when I think of my sins becoming white as snow.

> If we confess our sins, he is faithful and just and will forgive us our sins and purify us from all unrighteousness. (1 John 1:9)

Remember the thief who died on the cross alongside Jesus? He simply asked, "Jesus, remember me when you come into your kingdom." And Jesus accepted his repentant heart and promised to meet him in paradise (Luke 23:42–43).

God doesn't require perfection but "a broken and contrite heart" (Psalm 51:17). When we are genuinely sorry for our wrongs and ask for forgiveness, he forgives and promises to wash us—as white as country snow.

∞

Thank you, Father, for the beauty and simplicity of your forgiveness.

50

The Road to Heaven

DOREEN BLOMSTRAND

*For here we do not have an enduring city, but we
are looking for the city that is to come.*

HEBREWS 13:14

Eight-year-old Trevor listened intently. His family was discussing plans to take a vacation together. They talked about flights and several destination possibilities, including Disneyland.

Soon after, Trevor's mom, Rhonda, tucked him in bed.

Trevor asked her, "Could we fly to heaven to see if we really like it before we die?"

His mom smiled and explained that we can't take a trip on a plane to heaven.

The rest of the family heard Rhonda laughing as she came back to join them. They were soon laughing with her over Trevor's idea of checking out heaven before deciding if he wants to go there.

Most of us wonder what heaven will really be like. In his autobiography *I Didn't Do It Alone*, Art Linkletter ponders, "I can't quite understand heaven as it is generally depicted by theologians. It sounds like the dullest place out of the world to me; I wouldn't want to be caught dead there. I've always thrived on work . . . I cannot imagine spending eternity wandering around in some pastel environment, listening to people sing and play the harp. I must believe that God in His infinite wisdom has figured out a different-strokes-for-different-folks situation."

He's right. Heaven is not the sitting-on-a-cloud-playing-a-harp life people tell jokes about.

> No eye has seen, no ear has heard, no mind has conceived what God has prepared for those who love him. (1 Corinthians 2:9)

Life is a series of choices. We don't have to know all the details; we just have to choose the right road. The Bible is our road map, and John 3:16 holds the promise:

> For God so loved the world that he gave his one and only Son, that whoever believes in him shall not perish but have eternal life.

⁓

Father, thank you that you've shown us the way to heaven. Help us make the choice that will put us on the right road. Then one day we will see you and experience all the wonderful plans you have for us.

Has God whispered to you through the spontaneous words of a child? Have your kid's delightful remarks made you smile? Maybe unexpected words from a grandparent or a teacher, or even a stranger you chatted with while standing in line, made you pause and ponder a life lesson. We're working on our next book; we'd love to hear your stories and comments. Please e-mail us at growingtowardGod@kregel.com.

DOREEN AND BARBARA